Published By Robert Corbin

@ Clarence Nixon

The Dukan Diet: Easy and Delicious Consolidation

and to Help You Lose Weight

All Right RESERVED

ISBN 978-87-94477-30-7

TABLE OF CONTENTS

Chicken And Vegetable Skewers 1

Rolls Of Smoked Salmon And Spinach 4

Oat Bran Toast 6

Scrambled Eggs With Herbs 8

Turkey Chunks 10

Spinach Omelet 11

Pan-Fried Lemon Broccoli 14

"Creamy" Chicken Soup 15

Peanut Butter Smoothie 17

Spinach Smoothie 18

Leek, Turkey Bacon And Gruyere Crust-Less Quiche 19

Homemade Oat Bran Cereal 22

Spanish Shrimp With Tamarind 24

- Herbed Cod Parcels 26
- Biscuit Roll "Condensed Milk" (For 1 Day) According To Dukan 28
- Biscuit Cake According To Dukan / Pp 33
- Whole Chicken Slow Cooker 38
- Insalata Caprese 39
- Chocolate Oat Bran Muffins 41
- Cinnamon Oat Bran Muffins 43
- Garlic And Tomato Marinated Grilled Shrimp 45
- Lemon Marinated Grilled Salmon 47
- Dukan Oat Pancakes 49
- Cream Cheese Casserole 50
- Minutes To Prepare 51
- Creamy Surimi Salad 53
- Fried Cheese Chips 55

- Smoked Turkey Wrap 57
- Chicken Meatballs 58
- Zucchini Lasagna 60
- Stuffed Baked Tomatoes 62
- Eggplant Frittata 64
- Double Chocolate Mint Cookies 65
- Oil-Free Chocolate Muffins | Plant-Based Desserts 69
- Oat Bran Galette 71
- Offe Frap Attack 72
- Beef Carpaccio With Arugula And Parmesan 73
- Bresaola Rolls With Fresh Cheese 76
- Smoked Salmon With Cucumber And Cottage Cheese 78
- Chocolate Oat Bran Muffins 81
- Zesty Lemon Pancakes 83

Tofu And Tomato Croutons 85

Shrimp Salad With Lemon And Parsley 87

Cream Of Cauliflower Soup 88

Ham And Vegetable Soup... 90

Pistachios Ice-Cream 92

Vanilla Ice-Cream... 94

French Toast With Strawberry Jam And Turkey Sausages 96

Strawberry Yoghurt Cake 99

Spicy Dukan Shrimp.. 101

Currywurst With Pumpkin Fries 104

Turkey Stew.. 107

Cottage Cheese Easter With Boiled Egg Yolks........ 109

Delicious Cutlets With Cottage Cheese According 112

Cajun Spice Mix 115

- Grilled Asparagus 117
- Dukan Bread 118
- Fast And Easy Ginger Dukan Biscuits 120
- Shrimp And Grits With Tasso Ham 122
- Lemon Chicken Grilled 125
- Oat Bran Dukan Porridge 127
- Sausage Scramble With Jalapenos 129
- Candice's Modified Dukan Diet Chocolate Muffins 130
- Crispy Chicken 132
- Meatballs In Tomato Sauce 134
- Scallops In Ham Wrap 137
- General Tso's Chicken 139
- Dukan Chili 141

Chicken And Vegetable Skewers

Ingredients:

- 1 courgette

- wooden skewers (soaked in water to prevent them from burning during cooking)

- Salt and pepper (to taste)

- 1 diced chicken breast

- 1 bell pepper (preferably of a different color)

- 1 red onion

- Spices (to taste, for example paprika, cumin, oregano).

Directions:

1. Prepare the Ingredients: Cut the chicken breast into similar sized cubes. Cut the bell pepper, red onion and courgettes into pieces large enough to thread onto the skewers.
2. Prepare the Vegetables and Chicken: Season the diced chicken with salt, pepper and your choice of spices.
3. Cut the vegetables into pieces large enough to thread onto the skewers.
4. Assemble the skewers: Thread the chicken pieces and vegetables alternately onto the wooden skewers.
5. You can create different combinations, such as chicken-pepper-onion-courgettes, or you can customize the order to your liking.
6. Cooking the kebabs: Cook the kebabs on a hot grill or oven grill, turning them occasionally to ensure even cooking.

7. The cooking time will depend on the size of the pieces and your personal preference for doneness of the chicken.
8. Make sure the chicken is cooked through and the vegetables are tender but crunchy.
9. Service: Once cooked, remove the skewers from the grill and let them rest for a few minutes.
10. You can serve the kebabs hot as an appetizer or as part of a main meal. Accompany the kebabs with a low-fat sauce or herb yogurt dip if you like.

Rolls Of Smoked Salmon And Spinach

Ingredients:

- 50g of fresh cheese (for example, ricotta or light spreadable cheese)
- Lemon juice
- Black pepper (to taste)
- 4 slices of smoked salmon
- 50g of fresh spinach
- Fresh herbs (for example, parsley or basil) for garnish (optional).

Directions:

1. Prepare the Ingredients: Thoroughly wash the fresh spinach and dry it. Cut the fresh cheese into thin slices. Squeeze the lemon juice.

2. Roll Out the Salmon Slices: Arrange the salmon slices on a clean work surface, overlapping them slightly.
3. Add the spinach and cheese: Spread the fresh spinach over the salmon slices, covering them evenly. Place the cheese slices on top of the spinach.
4. Season and Roll: Drizzle lemon juice over spinach and cheese filling. Add some freshly ground black pepper to taste. Gently roll up the salmon slices to form tight rolls.
5. Slice and Serve: Cut the smoked salmon and spinach rolls into sized pieces to enjoy as an appetizer. If you like, you can garnish with fresh herbs like parsley or basil to add a touch of freshness.
6. Service: Arrange the smoked salmon and spinach rolls on a serving plate and serve as a light and tasty appetizer.

Oat Bran Toast

Ingredients:

- 5 tbsp oat bran

- 3 egg whites

- 3 tbsp zero-fat yogurt

Directions:

1. In a bowl, beat the egg whites well – so they become slightly airy.
2. To this, add oat bran and yogurt – stir well.
3. In a non-stick pan, heat a bit of oil and place four round egg rings in it.
4. Divide the egg and oat bran mix into these rings.
5. Once the bottom side is fully cooked, remove them from the rings. Then, proceed to cook the other side.

6. Flatten each piece by applying some pressure count to ten – do not press on it for too long.
7. Once the toast is ready, grill – do so till both sides are brown. (This can be eaten hot or cold.)

Scrambled Eggs With Herbs

Ingredients:

- 2 scallions, finely sliced

- ¼ tbsp coriander, chopped

- ¼ tbsp fresh parsley, chopped

- 2 tbsp skimmed milk

- 3 eggs

- ¼ tbsp fresh chives, chopped

Directions:

1. In a bowl, mix the skimmed milk, eggs, scallions and herbs. Beat the mixture till the yolks are well mixed.
2. Place it in the microwave that is on full power – for about 45 seconds.

3. Remove it from the microwave – stir to mix again. Place it in the microwave for 15 seconds.
4. Repeat this till the eggs achieve the consistency you think is perfect.

Turkey Chunks

Ingredients:

- Juice of half a lemon

- 1 teaspoon spices (paprika, cumin)

- Salt and pepper to taste

- 2 slices of turkey breast

- 1 teaspoon extra virgin olive oil

- Basil leaves for garnish (optional)

Directions:

1. Cut slices of turkey breast into bite-sized pieces. In a bowl, mix the extra virgin olive oil, lemon juice, spices, salt, and pepper to create a marinade.

2. Add the turkey chunks to the marinade and mix well to coat them evenly. Let marinate for at least 10 minutes. Heat a nonstick skillet over medium-high heat.
3. Add the marinated turkey bites to the skillet and cook for 5 to 6 minutes per side or until golden brown and fully cooked through.
4. Garnish with basil leaves (if desired). Serve the turkey bites hot.

Spinach Omelet

Ingredients:

- 1 small onion, chopped

- 1 teaspoon extra virgin olive oil

- 4 eggs

- 100 g fresh spinach, washed and chopped

- Salt and pepper to taste.

Directions:

1. In a nonstick skillet, heat extra virgin olive oil over medium heat.
2. Add the chopped onion and chopped spinach to the pan and cook for 2-3 minutes, until the spinach wilts and the onion becomes translucent. In a bowl, beat the eggs with the salt and pepper.
3. Pour the beaten eggs into the skillet over the spinach and onion.
4. Cook the omelet over medium-low heat for 5-6 minutes or until the bottom solidifies.

5. Using a lid or plate, flip the omelet and cook for another 5-6 minutes until fully cooked. Cut the frittata into wedges or cubes and serve hot.

Pan-fried lemon broccoli

Ingredients:

- 3 garlic cloves, chopped

- 2-3 tbsp. lemon juice

- 1 bunch broccoli

- Salt and pepper to taste

Directions:

1. Wash and break the broccoli into small florets. Pan fry the broccoli and garlic together on high heat for about 1-2 minutes.
2. Be sure to stir constantly so mixture does not burn. Take pan off heat and cover.
3. Allow to steam for 5 minutes. Season with lemon juice, salt and pepper.

"Creamy" Chicken Soup

Ingredients:

- Pinch of black pepper

- 3 chicken breasts

- ½ lemon for seasoning

- 2-3 tbsp. oat bran

- ½ large yellow onion

- 2 garlic cloves

- Pinch of salt

- Pinch of thyme

Directions:

1. Place 2 ½ -3 cups of water into a saucepan to boil. Put all Ingredients: in pan except oats bran.
2. Cook on high heat for 10 minutes, and lower heat to simmer. Continue to cook for 20 minutes.
3. Add oat bran. Blend soup in blender or food processor. Serve hot.

Peanut Butter Smoothie

Ingredients:

- 1 tablespoon flax seeds
- 1 cup almond milk
- 1 tsp vanilla extract
- 2 cups banana
- 2 tablespoon peanut butter

Directions:
1. In a blender place all Ingredients: and blend until smooth
2. Pour smoothie in a glass and serve

Spinach Smoothie

Ingredients:

- 2 cups spinach

- 2 chia seeds

- 2 cups banana

- 2 cups strawberries

Directions:

1. In a blender place all Ingredients: and blend until smooth
2. Pour smoothie in a glass and serve

Leek, Turkey Bacon And Gruyere Crust-Less Quiche

Ingredients:

- 3/4 cup Gruyere cheese, grated

- 2 T Parmesan cheese, grated

- 3/4 cup 1% milk

- 1 1/2 cups egg substitute

- 1 t salt, 1/2 t pepper

- 2 medium leeks, white parts only, halved, rinsed well and sliced 1/4 inch thick

- 8 slices turkey bacon

- olive oil spray

- Pinch freshly grated nutmeg

Directions:

1. Put leeks in a large skillet with water to cover and a teaspoon salt.
2. Simmer over medium heat until the leeks are tender, between 5 and 6 minutes.
3. Drain and place back in the skillet and brown for a few minutes using a little bit of olive oil spray.
4. Remove the leeks and brown the turkey bacon, until just crisp. Transfer to paper towels to drain.
5. Spray a 9-inch glass or pie pan with olive oil and sprinkle the grated Parmesan evenly on top. Put pan on a baking sheet.
6. Whisk the milk and egg whites together and season with salt, pepper, and nutmeg.
7. Spread half the gruyere evenly in the pan, crumble the turkey bacon on top repeat with remaining cheese and leeks.

8. Pour egg mixture over the cheeses and bacon. Bake at 350 until the quiche is just set in the center, about 45 minutes. Serve warm or at room temperature.

Homemade Oat Bran Cereal

Ingredients:

- 1 tbsp sweetener (or less to your preference)

- 1 tsp cinnamon or cocoa, vanilla or the flavoring of your liking. I have used cinnamon and fat reduced cocoa so far. Both delicious.

- 2 tbsp oat bran

- 1 tbsp wheat bran

- 1 tbsp 0% fat quark

Directions:

1. Mix everything in a bowl and then spread on a baking paper with a spatula to create a thin layer of 3-4 millimeters.

2. Bake in the oven for about 20 mins or a bit more if you want them a bit more crispy and darker.
3. Let it cool for 10-15 mins and then break it to little pieces using your hands.

Spanish Shrimp With Tamarind

Ingredients:

- 1/2 roasted onion

- 5 pasilla chilies

- 3 drops of oil

- Salt

- 1 tsp chicken bouillon 0% fat

- 1/2 kg large shrimp

- 1 roasted and peeled tomato

- 2 cloves of roasted garlic

- 2 tbsp tamarind pulp or concentrate with no added sugar

Directions:

1. Roast the tomatoes and peel them, then handle the peppers, remove the seeds and remójalos in some hot water.
2. Peel and clean the shrimp, removing the vein and discarding the heads and tails.
3. Blend the tomatoes with the garlic, onion and chillies with a little water in which they were soaked. Strain.
4. In a heated nonstick pan, pour the sauce.
5. Let fry until well seasoned. Add salt, broth and tamarind.
6. Separately, with 3 drops of oil in a nonstick skillet, fry until shrimp begin to turn pink and pour into the sauce.
7. Wait a little boil, turn off and serve.

Herbed Cod Parcels

Ingredients:

- 4 sprigs of tarragon

- ½ lemon, juiced

- 1 red pepper, cut into small cubes

- 1 yellow pepper, cut into small cubes

- 4 fillets of cod

- 4 shallots, peeled and thinly sliced

- 1 teaspoon of olive oil

- 4 sprigs of parsley

- 4 sprigs of coriander

- Salt and pepper

Directions:

1. Brown shallots in a non-stick pan with the olive oil for 4 minutes.
2. Wash and dry the herbs and roughly chop them, then mix with the shallots.
3. Cut 4 rectangles of parchment paper.
4. Place the cod fillets on top and season with salt and pepper, cover with the shallot-herb mix and a few drops of lemon juice.
5. Close the paper around the fish to make parcels and put onto oven trays.
6. Cook in the oven for 10 minutes at 425° F.
7. After removing them from the oven, let rest for 5 minutes. Serve the peppers alongside the parcels.

Biscuit Roll "Condensed Milk" (For 1 Day)
According To Dukan

Ingredients:

For the biscuit:

- 2 tbsp COM20 gr2/3 DOP
- 1 tbsp cornstarch20 gr1 extra
- 5 eggs
- 2 tbsp soft curdwith a slide
- 2 tsp baking powder
- 2 tbsp oat branground into flour
- 1.5 tbsp wheat branground into flour
- 1 tsp flax seed(ground into flour)
- sucrose

- A pinch of salt

For cream:

- 200 ml. Skimmed milk0.5-1.5%

- 3 yolks

- 1 tbsp com10 gr1/3 dop

- Sucrose

- Aromatic "condensed milk"if there

Directions:

1. From the very beginning, we will prepare the condensed milk cream.
2. Add the yolks to the milk, pour in the catfish and stir well so that there are no lumps. Add sugar.
3. We put on a small fire and boil until thick, stirring occasionally. Remove from fire and leave to cool.

4. For the biscuit, beat the eggs until they double in volume. Beat at maximum power for 10 minutes, no less.
5. Without turning off the mixer and continuing to beat, add sucrose.
6. In a different bowl, mix it all the dry ingredients: and sift them, so the bran and flax seeds should be crushed as much as possible.
7. Continuing to beat the eggs, add the cottage cheese in a spoon, and then gradually add the dry mixture, but not all at once!
8. That is, they added a spoon-whipped, another spoon-whipped, and so on. As a result, we get a fairly liquid homogeneous dough.
9. Pour the dough onto a baking sheet On a silicone or teflon mat, or parchment lightly oiled

10. The pan is large, standard size. Bake at 180 c for 12-15 minutes. The dough should be browned on top.
11. Don't let the dough dry out! Remove the finished biscuit from the mat and lay it on a clean kitchen towel. Together with a towel we turn the biscuit into a roll and let it cool completely.
12. We unfold the cooled biscuit, cut off the dry edges. Lubricate the entire surface with cooled cream (leave one spoonful of cream) and roll into a loose roll. Lubricate the roll with the remaining cream on top and decorate with the crushed remains of the cake.
13. We send it to the refrigerator for impregnation. Better to leave overnight. And in the morning you will get an amazing biscuit roll! Big roll for 1 day!

14. Wonderful biscuit and very juicy cream! Treat yourself!

Biscuit Cake According To Dukan / Pp

Ingredients:

For the biscuit:

- 100 gr soft fat-free cottage cheesecreamy

- 1 tsp baking powder

- 1 tsp lime or lemon zest

- my morningliquid 1.5 cap

- a pinch of salt

- 4 tbsp oat bran60 gr

- 4-5 tbsp skimmed milk powder (SOM)60 gr

- 2 whole eggs

- 2 egg whites

- 1 tbsp cornstarch 20 gr 1 BALL

- 1 tbsp any whole wheat flour (I use oatmeal) 20 gr 1 BALL

- Aromatic "Cognac"/"Rum" + "Cupcake"/"Biscuit"

- If there are no flavors, add vanillin for flavor

For GLAZE:

- 2 yolks

- 4-5 tbsp skimmed milk powder (SOM) 60 gr

- 1 tbsp lime or lemon juice

- saharzam

Directions:

1. Prepare all the Ingredients:.

2. Sift all dry Ingredients: through a sieve, except for bran. Then add bran, sucrose, cottage cheese
3. If you use any fillers - put them right now
4. Divide the eggs into proteins and yolks. For the test, we need 4 proteins, 2 yolks
5. That is! We have 4 eggs in total. 4 whites and 2 yolks go to the dough, leave the remaining 2 yolks for glaze
6. Add the yolks to the dough, beat the whites well with a pinch of salt until strong peaks (there should be a spoon in the whites)
7. Beat the dough until smooth with a mixer, add aromatics, beat again.
8. Introduce proteins into the dough in several parts. Gently fold egg whites inside the batter until completely combined.
9. We spread it in molds, I have 2 paper molds with a diameter of 9 cm (pre-lubricate them with a drop of oil)

10. Bake at 180C for 20-25 minutes without convection! We check the readiness with a toothpick, there should be no raw dough left on it
11. After baking, turn off the oven and leave the cakes in it for 10-15 minutes. We do this so that the Easter cakes do not "blow away", but remain magnificent.
12. While the Easter cakes are "resting" in the oven, we make the glaze.
13. I remove the film from the yolks. To them we add lime or lemon juice, sucrose, mix everything.
14. Now, in parts, we introduce the pre-sifted SOM to the required consistency. The icing should have a consistency similar to thick condensed milk.
15. We apply icing on still warm Easter cakes, sprinkle with sprinkles immediately. Place in

the refrigerator until the frosting is completely cool and set.

16. This glaze does not crack, hardens well and does not smear.
17. Easter cakes according to Dukan prepared according to this Directions: are very tender, airy and very tasty!

Whole Chicken Slow Cooker

Ingredients:

- 1 teaspoon onion powder
- 1 teaspoon ground thyme
- 1 teaspoon ground white pepper
- ½ teaspoon garlic powder
- ½ teaspoon ground black pepper
- 4 teaspoons salt, or to taste
- 2 teaspoons paprika
- 1 teaspoon cayenne pepper
- 1 whole whole chicken

Directions:

1. Mix salt, paprika, cayenne pepper, onion powder, thyme, white pepper, garlic powder, and black pepper together in a small bowl.
2. Rub seasoning mixture over the entire chicken to evenly season. Put rubbed chicken into a large resealable plastic bag refrigerate 8 hours to overnight.
3. Remove chicken from bag and cook in slow cooker on Low until no longer pink at the bone and the juices run clear, 4 to 8 hours.
4. An instant-read thermometer inserted into the thickest part of the thigh, near the bone should read 165 degrees F (74 degrees C).

Insalata Caprese

Ingredients:

- ⅓ cup fresh basil leaves

- 3 tablespoons extra virgin olive oil

- ½ teaspoon fine sea salt to taste

- 4 large ripe tomatoes, sliced 1/4 inch thick

- 1 pound fresh mozzarella cheese, sliced 1/4 inch thick

- 1 pinch freshly ground black pepper to taste

Directions:

1. On a large platter, alternate and overlap the tomato slices, mozzarella cheese slices, and basil leaves.
2. Drizzle with olive oil. Season with sea salt and pepper.

Chocolate Oat Bran Muffins

Ingredients:

- 2 eggs

- 6 tablespoons of zero fat yogurt

- 1 teaspoon of baking powder

- 6 tablespoons of oat bran

- 4 teaspoons of reduced fat, no sugar added cocoa powder

- Sweetener to taste

Directions:

1. Mix all the dry Ingredients: in a bowl.
2. Add the yogurt and eggs and whisk until smooth.
3. Add sweetener to taste.

4. Divide the mixture equally between 6 paper muffin cases in a muffin tray.
5. Bake in a preheated oven at 350 degrees F for 15 to 18 minutes.

Cinnamon Oat Bran Muffins

Ingredients:

- 2 eggs
- 5 tablespoons of zero fat yogurt
- 1 teaspoon of baking powder
- 1 1/2 teaspoons of cinnamon.
- 6 tablespoons of oat bran
- Sweetener to taste

Directions:

1. Mix all the dry ingredients in a bowl.
2. Add the yogurt and eggs and whisk until smooth.
3. Add sweetener to taste.

4. Divide the mixture equally between 6 paper muffin cases in a muffin tray.
5. Bake in a preheated oven at 350 degrees F for 15 to 18 minutes.

Garlic And Tomato Marinated Grilled Shrimp

Ingredients:

- 2 tablespoons chopped fresh basil

- ½ teaspoon salt

- ¼ teaspoon cayenne pepper

- 2 pounds fresh shrimp, peeled and de-veined

- 3 cloves garlic, minced

- 1/3 cup olive oil

- ¼ cup tomato sauce

- 2 tablespoons red wine vinegar

- Skewers

Directions:

1. Put together all Ingredients: except shrimp. Combine all Ingredients: until you create a perfectly blended mixture.
2. Add the shrimp, and make sure to coat each shrimp evenly. Allow the spices to penetrate the shrimp by setting aside the mixture.
3. Cover the bowl, and then refrigerate for 30 minutes to an hour. You can also mix the shrimp into the sauce once in a while during the marinating period.
4. Put the shrimp in the skewers. Apply oil on the grill grate before grilling the shrimp, so it doesn't stick. Cook the shrimp for two to three minutes over the grill.
5. Remove from grill and place on serving platter. Serve, and enjoy!

Lemon Marinated Grilled Salmon

Ingredients:

- 1/3 cup soy sauce

- 1/3 cup brown sugar

- 1/3 cup water

- 1 ½ pounds salmon fillet

- Lemon pepper to taste

- Garlic powder to taste

- Salt to taste

- ¼ cup vegetable oil

Directions:

1. Rub salmon fillets with salt, lemon pepper, and garlic powder.

2. Prepare the soy sauce mixture by adding together brown sugar, soy sauce, water, and oil.
3. Make sure to completely dissolve the sugar. In a re-sealable bag, put together pre-seasoned fish fillets and soy sauce. Roll over the fish fillet, so that it is fully covered with the soy sauce mixture. Refrigerate for two hours.
4. Grease the grill grates with oil before grilling the fillets. Cook each side until fish meat can be separated easily when you put a fork into it.
5. Remove from grill, and transfer to a serving platter.
6. Serve, and enjoy!

Dukan Oat Pancakes

Ingredients:

- 1 1/2 tbsp. quark (cheddar, new corrosive set)

- 1 egg, large

- 1 1/2 tbsp. grain, oat

Directions:

1. Pour oat grain in medium bowl. Add egg and quark.
2. Mix fixings well. Pour onto pre-lubed non-stick pan.
3. Cook for a few minutes for each side. Serve.

Cream Cheese Casserole

Ingredients:

- 8 ounces of cream cheddar, fat-free

- 2 jars of sickle rolls, diminished fat

- 1 pound of seared sausage

Directions:

1. Spread 1 would bow rolls on the lower part of a 13x9-inch be able to container. Squeeze the seams.
2. Cover the spread rolls with cream cheddar and sausage.
3. Spread other would bow rolls on top of wiener and cream be able to cheddar blend. Heat utilizing Directions: on bundle. Serve.

Minutes To Prepare

Ingredients:

- 3 tbsp Oatbran

- 1-2 egg whites

- 1 stock cube

- Crushed chilli (if you want it spicy)

- 500g Lean minced beef or turkey mince

- You can add other herbs and/or spices as you want..

Directions:

1. Put mince into a bowl and stir in the crushed stock cube and oatbran
2. Add the egg whites and mix together until all the egg has been absorbed (it should form

into a compact mixture, not too sticky, if it is too sticky mix in a sprinkle of oatbran)
3. Then mix in the spices/herbs (add whatever spices you like to the mix.)
4. Take lumps of the mixture and with your hands make into 6 patties and grill on a medium heat for 10-20 minutes turning in between.

Creamy Surimi Salad

Ingredients:

- 100g Surimi, thawed and cold (cut into bitesize chunks)

- 185g can Tuna in Brine or Springwater (drained, and flaked finely)

For THE CREAMY SAUCE:

- 1/4 tsp. Mustard powder

- 1/4 tsp. Garlic powder

- 1/4 tsp. Hot chili pepper sauce

- 3 Tbs. Lowfat PLAIN Yogurt (less than 2%)

- 1 tsp. Worcestershire sauce

- Zest of half a lemon + 1 tsp. Freshly squeezed Lemon juice

- Pepper (optional)

Directions:

1. Mix cold Surimi and tuna together well in bowl and set aside.
2. Mix all Ingredients: for sauce until combined evenly then add to Surimi and Tuna and mix well until the whole mixture is evenly covered in creamy mixture.
3. Season with pepper and serve immediately.

Fried Cheese Chips

Ingredients:

- 1 spray of oil

- 1 teaspoon of garlic powder

- 1 pack of tofu (extra hard)

- 2 tablespoons of white cheddar (skimmed)

Directions:

1. Preheat the oven to 200 degrees.
2. Dry the tofu with a paper towel.
3. Cut it into 1/2 inch thick slices.
4. Use a paper towel to get rid of extra water on each slice.
5. Spray a small amount of oil spray on baking paper and tofu and cook for 30 minutes.
6. Grate the cheddar cheese on them.
7. Cook some more.

8. Take it out of the oven, pour garlic powder on it and serve.

Smoked Turkey Wrap

Ingredients:

- 1 slice ham

- 3 eggs

- Curd cheese (0.5 cup)

- 3 smoked turkey

- 1 pinch of black seed

Directions:

1. Preheat the oven to 200 degrees.
2. Mix the curd cheese with the egg whites.
3. Spread the mixture between slices of smoked turkey and roll them.
4. Spread the egg yolk on it and sprinkle a little amount of black seed.
5. Bake for about 15 minutes until well browned.

Chicken Meatballs

Ingredients:

- 1 minced garlic clove, small
- 1 lb. Chicken, ground
- 1 egg, large
- 3 tbsp. Chopped dill or parsley
- Spices: kosher salt, ground pepper and garlic powder
- 1 chopped onion, small
- 2 tbsp. Bran, oat

Directions:

1. Preheat oven to 350F.
2. Mince garlic and onion.

3. Add all Ingredients: to large bowl. Mix them together well.
4. Form the mixture into 15 to 20 balls and place on a pan.
5. Bake in the middle rack of 350F oven for 18-20 minutes, till juices are running clear.
6. Remove from oven and serve.

Zucchini Lasagna

Ingredients:

- 7 oz. ground beef, lean

- 3 ½ oz. mozzarella cheese, light

- 1 tbsp. tomato extract, pure

- ½ onion, medium

- 3 ½ oz. turkey breast, smoked

- 1 garlic clove

- Oregano, chives, parsley, kosher salt and

- 2 lengthwise-sliced zucchinis, medium

- 2 peeled, de-seeded tomatoes, ripe, large

- Ground pepper

Directions:

1. Grill each side of sliced zucchinis in non-stick pan. Set aside.
2. Sauté onion and garlic in pan on low heat. Add kosher salt, ground pepper and beef. Cook on low.
3. Pour 1 ¾ oz. of filtered water in food processor. Add chives, parsley and tomatoes (diced). Combine till smooth.
4. Add sauce to beef. Add tomato extract. Boil mixture for 12-15 minutes.
5. Add some sauce to baking dish/pizza form for oven cooking. Form layers using zucchini, then turkey breast, then cheese and sauce. Repeat layers two times. Top with cheese and oregano.
6. Place in oven for 20-25 minutes. Then turn oven to off. Allow lasagna to sit for 12-15 minutes. Serve.

Stuffed Baked Tomatoes

Ingredients:

- 7 ounces extra-lean ham, finely chopped
- 2 tablespoons very finely chopped fresh basil
- 8 tomatoes
- Salt and freshly ground black pepper
- 4 eggs

Directions:

1. Preheat oven to 425°F.
2. Cut the tops off the tomatoes spoon out the insides, sprinkle a little salt inside, and turn them over on a plate to let their juices drain.

3. In a medium bowl, beat the eggs, season with salt and pepper to taste, and add the ham and basil.
4. Turn the tomatoes over and place them in a baking dish. Spoon the egg mixture into the tomatoes and bake for 25 minutes.

Eggplant Frittata

Ingredients:

- A pinch of ground nutmeg
- 3 sprigs of fresh thyme, chopped
- 3 sprigs of fresh rosemary, chopped
- ⅛ Teaspoon vegetable oil
- 14 ounces eggplant, peeled and cut into ½-inch slices
- Salt and freshly ground black pepper
- 3 eggs
- 1 cup fat-free milk

Directions:

1. Preheat oven to 300°F.

2. Place the eggplant slices in a colander, sprinkle them with a little salt and set them aside until their juices drain out, about 30 minutes.
3. Wipe the slices dry with a clean kitchen towel.
4. Bring a medium pot of water to a boil and blanch the eggplant for 5 minutes, then drain
5. In a medium bowl, mix the eggs, milk, nutmeg, thyme, rosemary, and salt and pepper to taste until thoroughly combined.
6. Coat a 9 × 9-inch baking dish with the oil and wipe out any excess with a paper towel.
7. Arrange the eggplant slices in the prepared baking dish and pour the egg mixture over the eggplant.
8. Bake for 30 minutes.

Double Chocolate Mint Cookies

Ingredients:

Wet

- 1/2 cup fresh mint, finely diced, OR 1.5 tsp mint extract

- 3 tbsp pure maple syrup

- 1 tsp apple cider vinegar

- 1.5 cups cooked chickpeas, OR 1 15 oz can (no salt added), drained and rinsed

- 1/4 cup almond butter, see notes

Dry

- 1/2 tsp baking soda

- 1/2 tsp salt

- 1/3 cup dairy-free chocolate chips

- 1/2 cup oat flour, see notes

- 3 tbsp cocoa powder, or cacao powder

- 3 tbsp date or coconut sugar

Directions:

1. Preheat oven to 350 degrees
2. Finely dice your fresh mint (if you are using mint extract, you can skip this step).
3. Add all wet Ingredients: to a food processor and pulse until chickpeas are broken down and well blended.
4. Add dry Ingredients: (except chocolate chips) to the food processor and pulse until wet and dry ingredients are well combined.
5. Fold in chocolate chips.
6. Line 2 baking sheets with parchment paper or a silicone baking mat.
7. Spoon mixture onto baking sheet in rounded tablespoon sized drops.
8. Wet fingers and shape cookies, flattening the tops slightly.

9. Transfer your baking sheets to the oven and bake for 12-14 minutes, until edges begin to look dry.
10. Let cookies cool on the baking sheet for about 5 mins before transferring to a wire rack for cooling.

Oil-Free Chocolate Muffins | Plant-Based Desserts

Ingredients:

- 6 tablespoons water
- 2 tablespoons ground flax seed heaping tablespoons
- 1 1/2 teaspoons baking powder
- 1 teaspoon arrowroot powder
- 1 teaspoon vanilla extract
- 1/4 teaspoon salt
- 15 ounces black beans can, without the liquid, or 1 3/4 cups cooked
- 3/4 cup cacao powder

- 1/2 cup coconut palm sugar heaping cup

- 1 banana small or 1/2 large

- 1/4 cup unsweetened applesauce

Directions:

1. Preheat oven to 350.
2. Puree all ingredients until smooth – the consistency should be less thick than frosting but not runny.
3. Spoon equal quantity of the mixture into baking cup liners in a 12 cup standard size muffin tin – cups should be about half full.
4. Bake 30 minutes at 350 degrees – muffin tops should be dry, slightly raised and cracked.
5. Let cool for at least 30 minutes then enjoy!

Oat Bran Galette

Ingredients:

- 3 tablespoons 0% fat Greek yogurt and

- 3 tablespoons oat bran.

- 2 egg whites

Directions:

1. Whisk together the Ingredients: in a bowl until you arrive at a smooth liquid batter. If it seems too thick, add more yogurt to thin out.
2. Grease the bottom of a non-stick pan lightly and pour in half of the batter, cooking on medium heat until both sides turn golden brown.
3. Repeat the process for the remaining half of the batter.

Offe Frap Attack

Ingredients:

- 16 ice cubes and

- 4 teaspoons aspartame.

- 1 cup skimmed milk straight from the fridge

- 1 cup strong black coffee or espresso, cold

Directions:

1. Blend the milk, coffee and sweetener in a blender until they become a nice, foamy mixture.
2. Blend the ice in until broken into small chunks.
3. After stirring well, pour into 2 tall glasses and enjoy!

Beef Carpaccio With Arugula And Parmesan

Ingredients:

- Lemon juice

- Extra virgin olive oil

- Salt and pepper (to taste)

- Parmesan flakes for garnish (optional)

- 100g of beef (fillet or sirloin) thin and well cleaned

- 40g of fresh arugula

- 20g of grated Parmesan cheese

- Slices of crusty bread to accompany (optional).

Directions:

1. Prepare the beef: Make sure you use high-quality beef that is tender and well trimmed. Place the meat in the freezer for about 30 minutes before slicing, to make it easier to slice thinly.
2. Slice the beef: With a sharp knife, cut the beef into very thin slices. You can do this by placing the meat on a cutting board and chopping it with firm motions. Try to get even slices.
3. Arrange the carpaccio: Take the slices of beef and arrange them on a serving plate so that they overlap slightly, creating a thin, even layer.
4. Seasonings: Squeeze a little lemon juice over the beef carpaccio to add freshness and a slight acidic aftertaste.
5. Drizzle a drizzle of extra virgin olive oil on the meat. Add salt and pepper to taste.
6. Add arugula and grana cheese: Spread the fresh arugula over the beef, covering it

evenly. Sprinkle the grated Parmesan cheese over the arugula. You can also add some flakes of grits for a more appealing presentation.
7. Garnish and service: If you wish, you can garnish the carpaccio with some additional parmesan flakes. Serve the beef carpaccio with arugula and parmesan as an appetizer. You can accompany it with slices of crusty bread.
8. Make sure you choose fresh, high-quality beef for best results. Also keep in mind that beef carpaccio is a raw dish, so it's important to make sure the Ingredients: are fresh and the beef has been handled properly to ensure food safety.

Bresaola Rolls With Fresh Cheese

Ingredients:

- 1 teaspoon of lemon juice
- Fresh herbs (for example, basil or parsley) finely chopped
- Ground black pepper (to taste)
- 4 slices of bresaola
- 100g of fresh cheese (for example, ricotta or light spreadable cheese)
- Fresh arugula for garnish (optional).

Directions:

1. Prepare the Ingredients: In a bowl, mix the fresh cheese with the lemon juice, the finely chopped aromatic herbs and the black

pepper. Make sure the mixture is well blended.
2. Spread the slices of bresaola: Arrange the slices of bresaola on a clean work surface, overlapping them slightly.
3. Filling the rolls: Take a generous portion of the fresh cheese mixture and spread it evenly over each slice of bresaola.
4. Roll up the rolls: Gently roll up each slice of bresaola with the fresh cheese filling, creating tight and compact rolls.
5. Garnish and service: If you wish, you can garnish the bresaola rolls with some fresh arugula leaves to add freshness and a touch of colour. Arrange the rollatini on a serving plate and serve as a light and tasty appetizer.
6. You can further customize the Directions: by adding other Ingredients: to the filling of the rollatini, such as chopped olives, sun-dried tomatoes or chopped walnuts, to enrich the

flavour. Experiment and adapt the Directions: to your personal tastes.

Smoked Salmon With Cucumber And Cottage Cheese

Ingredients:

- 1 cucumber

- Lemon juice

- Fresh herbs (for example, dill or parsley) finely chopped

- 2 slices of smoked salmon

- 50g of fresh cheese (for example, ricotta or light spreadable cheese)

- Salt and pepper (to taste).

Directions:

1. Prepare the Ingredients: Wash the cucumber and cut it into thin slices. Finely chop the fresh herbs.
2. Roll Out the Salmon Slices: Arrange the salmon slices on a clean work surface.
3. Prepare the filling: In a bowl, mix the fresh cheese with the chopped aromatic herbs. Add a little lemon juice, salt and pepper to taste. Mix everything well to obtain a homogeneous mixture.
4. Salmon filling: Spread the cream cheese and herb mixture over the salmon slices, covering them evenly.
5. Add Cucumber: Place a few slices of cucumber on the bottom half of each salmon wedge. Roll the rolls: Gently roll the salmon with the fresh cheese and cucumber filling, creating tight and compact rolls.
6. Garnish and service: You can garnish the rollatini with some additional fresh herbs.

Arrange the smoked salmon rolls with cucumber and fresh cheese on a platter and serve them as a light and tasty appetizer.
7. You can further customize the Directions: by adding other Ingredients: like pink pepper, capers or extra lemon juice to vary the flavor. Make sure you choose high quality smoked salmon to get the best taste.

Chocolate Oat Bran Muffins

Ingredients:

- 12 tbsp zero-fat yogurt

- 8 tsp cocoa powder (Make sure this is reduced fat and has no sugar added)

- 1 tsp baking powder

- 4 eggs

- 12 tbsp oat bran

- Sweetener, according to taste

Directions:

1. Preheat oven at 350 °F.
   In a bowl, mix the cocoa powder, oat bran and baking powder together.

2. To this, add the eggs and yogurt – whisk till the resultant mixture becomes smooth and consistent.
3. Next, add sweetener according to your taste.
4. Divide the mixture into muffin cases placed in a muffin tray.
5. Bake for about 15 minutes, till the centre of the muffin is fully cooked.

Zesty Lemon Pancakes

Ingredients:

- 8 tbsp fat-free yogurt
- 4 tbsp sweetener
- Zest of a lemon
- 2 eggs
- 2 egg whites
- 2 tbsp oat bran

Directions:

1. In a bowl, beat the egg whites and eggs together.
2. To this, add oat bran, yogurt, sweetener and lemon zest – make sure you stir well.

3. In a non-stick pan, heat a few drops of oil – make sure it spreads to all corners of the pan.
4. Place some of the pancake batter onto the pan. Cook on medium heat, till bubbles form on the pancake.
5. Then, turn the pancake and continue letting it cook – till the pancake becomes brown in color.
6. Repeat the process till all of the batter has been us

Tofu And Tomato Croutons

Ingredients:

- 1 teaspoon extra virgin olive oil
- 1 clove of garlic, cut in half
- Salt and pepper to taste
- Fresh basil for garnish (optional)
- 100 g firm tofu, thinly sliced
- 4 slices of whole wheat bread
- 1 ripe tomato, diced

Directions:

1. Heat a nonstick skillet over medium-high heat. Add the tofu slices to the pan and cook them for 2-3 minutes per side, until lightly browned.

2. Toast the slices of whole wheat bread in a toaster oven or under the oven grill. Rub garlic cut in half on the toasted bread slices.
3. In a bowl, mix diced tomatoes with extra virgin olive oil, salt, and pepper. Arrange the tofu slices on the toasted bread slices.
4. Add the seasoned tomatoes on top of the tofu. Garnish with fresh basil leaves (if desired). Serve the tofu and tomato croutons as an appetizer.

Shrimp Salad With Lemon And Parsley

Ingredients:

- Juice of 1 lemon

- Chopped fresh parsley

- 200 g shelled and boiled shrimp

- Salt and pepper (optional)

Directions:

1. In a bowl, mix the boiled shrimp with the lemon juice. Add chopped parsley and mix well.
2. Add salt and pepper to taste, if desired. Let the shrimp salad rest in the refrigerator for at least 30 minutes. Serve the shrimp salad as an appetizer.

Cream Of Cauliflower Soup

Ingredients:

- ½ tsp. nutmeg (optional)
- 1 onion
- 2 tbsp. parsley (finely chopped)
- ½ tsp. salt
- 2 tbsp. skim milk
- 1 head cauliflower, chopped into small pieces
- 2 c. chicken broth
- 2 garlic cloves
- ½ tsp. white pepper

Directions:

1. In a large pot, bring cauliflower, broth and milk to a boil. Add onion and garlic.
2. Cook until tender. Add salt, pepper, nutmeg and parsley before serving.

Ham And Vegetable Soup

Ingredients:

- 2 tbsp. fat-free quark

  3 slices turkey ham

- ½ c. fresh basil, coarsely chopped

- 1 large yellow onion

- 1 can tomatoes

- 3 cloves garlic, minced

- About 1 ¾ c. vegetable stock

Directions:

1. Heat a saucepan, and add a little bit of water. Add garlic and onions and sauté for few minutes.

2. Add canned tomatoes and stir, crushing the tomatoes with spoon. Add vegetable stock. Stir and add sliced ham and basil.
3. Cook on low heat for around 40 minutes. Serve topped with quark and fresh basil.

Pistachios Ice-Cream

Ingredients:

- 1 cup sugar
- 1 vanilla bean
- 1 tsp almond extract
- 1 cup cherries
- 4 egg yolks
- 1 cup heavy cream
- 1 cup milk
- ½ Cup pistachios

Directions:

1. In a saucepan whisk together all Ingredients:
2. Mix until bubbly

3. Strain into a bowl and cool
4. Whisk in favorite fruits and mix well
5. Cover and refrigerate for 2-3 hours
6. Pour mixture in the ice-cream maker and follow manufacturer Directions:
7. Serve when ready

Vanilla Ice-Cream

Ingredients:

- 1 cup heavy cream
- 1 cup brown sugar
- 1 tablespoon corn syrup
- 1 cup milk
- 1 tablespoon cornstarch
- 1 oz. Cream cheese
- 1 vanilla bean

Directions:

1. In a saucepan whisk together all Ingredients:
2. Mix until bubbly
3. Strain into a bowl and cool

4. Whisk in favorite fruits and mix well
5. Cover and refrigerate for 2-3 hours
6. Pour mixture in the ice-cream maker and follow manufacturer Directions:
7. Serve when ready

French Toast With Strawberry Jam And Turkey Sausages

Ingredients:

French toast

- 2 Slices of Whole Wheat Bread

- 1 Egg

- 1/3 Cup of Non-Fat Milk

- Cinnamon

- Salt

Turkey "sausages"

- 1/2 lb of Turkey (Makes 4)

- Thyme

- Salt and Pepper

- Strawberry Jam

- 2 Handfuls of Strawberries (consolidation only allows for 1 serving but you won't be using all the jam in one sitting)

- Sweetener

- 2 Tbsp. of Lemon

Directions:

1. Mix together ground turkey with thyme, salt and pepper. Shape into small patties and "fry" using Pam.
2. While patties are cooking, prepare strawberry jam. Dice strawberries, add sugar, and lemon juice. Put on low heat until it reduces to a jam consistency.
3. Prepare egg mixture with milk, dash of cinnamon and a pinch of salt. Quickly soak

your piece of bread and put in pan for about 3 minutes on each side (or until brown).
4. Serve french toast with the strawberry jam and a dollop of fat free sour cream

Strawberry Yoghurt Cake

Ingredients:

- 3tbsp natural yoghurt/strawberry yoghurt

- 3 eggs

- 100g strawberry yoghurt fat free

- 6tbsp oat bran

- 6tbsp skimmed milk

- 3tbsp sweetener

- 1tsp baking powder

Directions:

1. Simply mix everything together - it is like a runny batter mix. Line the inside of a loaf tin with baking parchment/paper

2. Or even better pour straight in to a silicon baking tray. Put in a COLD oven, and bake on 180C, Gas 4 for 35 mins. Leave for a while, then turn out and leave to cool.
3. You can change the flavour of the cake by adding different flavoured yogurt and essences. I have seen some people also make muffins with this recipe. If you have a pound shop near you

Spicy Dukan Shrimp

Ingredients:

- 1 tablespoon sriracha
- 1/2 teaspoon chipotle powder
- 1 teaspoon ground cumin
- Freshly ground sea salt and pepper, to taste
- 1 tablespoon nonfat greek yogurt
- 1 tablespoon nonfat cottage cheese
- 1 pound prawns, shelled and deveined with the shrimp cleaner
- 1/2 jalapeno, shaved paper-thin with a ceramic slicer

- 1 lemon, zested with the better zester and juiced with the citrus press

- 1 tablespoon brandy2 cloves garlic, minced with the garlic rocker

- Chives, "chopped" with the herb scissors

Directions:

1. Put prawns in a Lékué Steamcase shave jalapeno over prawns in Steamcase.
2. Put lemon juice and zest, brandy, garlic, Sriracha and spices in a QuicKMix, and shake until blended.
3. Pour mix over prawns and stir in.
4. Let sit for at least an hour in the refrigerator
5. While the prawns are marinating, blend the nonfat yogurt and the nonfat cottage until very smooth to make the Faux Fromage Frais refrigerate

6. Microwave prawns in Steamcase for 2 minutes at 1000W power (if your microwave is higher wattage, use a lower power percentage.)
7. Stir and microwave another 3 minutes at 1000W power. Let sit for 1 minute.
8. Remove prawns to 2 plates and whisk Faux Fromage Frais into the sauce that's left in the Steamcase.
9. Spoon sauce over prawns. Sprinkle with chopped chives. Wish that you could have some bread or rice to sop up the extra sauce!

Currywurst with Pumpkin Fries

Ingredients:

- 1 pinch of paprika
- 1 dash of Tabasco sauce for the pumpkin fries:
- 300 g of pumpkin
- 1 tbsp. cornstarch
- 3 drops of olive oil
- 1 pinch of salt and pepper
- 1 dash of curry powder
- low fat sausage (3% fat) for the curry sauce:
- ¼ onion
- 100 g of diced tomatoes

- 2 drops honey flavouringl

- 1 tbsp vinegar

- 1 tbsp low fat bouillon cube (chicken or vegetable)

- 1 tbsp soy sauce

- 1 tablespoon curry powder

- 1 tbsp rosemary parchment paper

Directions:

1. For the pumpkin fries: Preheat oven to 190 ° C. Cover a baking sheet with parchment paper.
2. Cut the pumpkin into strips like fries. Mix in a large bowl cornstarch, olive oil, salt, pepper, curry and rosemary.
3. Add the fried pumpkin and mix well to flavor the fries.

4. Place the fries on a baking sheet in a single layer and bake 25 to 30 minutes.
5. Halfway through (10-15 minutes), turn fries and continue cooking.
6. For the curry sauce: Peel the onion and chop finely.
7. Place all Ingredients: in a blender and puree. Pour into a saucepan and simmer for 5 minutes over medium heat.
8. For the sausages: Fry the sausages in a pan on all sides.
9. Finally, cut the sausages into chunks, pour the curry sauce over, sprinkle with half tbsp curry and serve with pumpkin fries. Enjoy while it's hot!
10. Tip: If you are really hungry, it is possbile to prepare an oat bran galette to accompany this dish.

Turkey Stew

Ingredients:

- 4 tomatoes, cut into pieces

- 1 tablespoon of tomato puree diluted in ¼ cup of water.

- 2 tablespoons of white wine

- 2 shallots

- 2 cloves of garlic

- 3 lbs of turkey breast, cut into pieces

- 1 lb of mushrooms, cut into pieces

- 4 large carrots, cut into pieces

- 1 pinch of salt and pepper

Directions:

1. Place turkey in a casserole dish and add mushrooms, carrots and tomatoes.
2. Add tomato puree, white wine, shallots, garlic cloves, basil, salt and pepper.
3. Cover the casserole dish and leave to cook on a medium heat for 30 minutes.

Cottage Cheese Easter With Boiled Egg Yolks

Ingredients:

- 1 tsp lime (lemon) zest

- 1-2 tbsp lime (lemon) juice

- 50 ml (+/-) skimmed milk(liquid)

- 500 gr fat-free cottage cheese(i have grainy, you can take it from the pack)

- 4 pcs boiled yolks

- 60 gr skimmed milk powder(com)

- 30 gr coconut oil(or any other unscented)   (norm for 2 days)

- Sucrose

- Vanillin

- For filling: nuts, berries, raisins, candied fruits, etc.

Directions:

1. At the beginning of cooking, melt and cool the coconut oil
2. Grind cottage cheese through a sieve. If you can't do this, beat the cottage cheese until smooth with a blender or pass through a meat grinder
3. Grind boiled yolks through a sieve to cottage cheese
4. Add the rest of the Ingredients:, sift the SOM through a sieve
5. Add a little liquid milk and interrupt with a blender. If the mass is too thick, add a little more milk.
6. If you use cottage cheese from a pack, liquid milk may not be needed at all
7. Add the selected filling. I use ground hazelnuts

8. Wet 3 layers of gauze and wring out. We spread the cheesecloth evenly in the paster so that the edges hang down
9. We spread the curd mass in the pastry box, put a saucer / board / lid from the container on top, put oppression
10. Leave in the refrigerator overnight, it is better to leave for a day. Periodically check Easter and drain the separated liquid
11. After the lapse of time, we take out Easter from the beekeeper and decorate as desired
12. Easter prepared in this way turns out to be very juicy, tender and fragrant!
13. Has a silky texture and pleasant acidity

Delicious Cutlets With Cottage Cheese

According

Ingredients:

- 1 egg(co categories)

- 2 medium onions

- Salt

- Spices to taste

- Greens to taste

- 1 tsp frying oils

- 400 gr ground beef(or any other)

- 200 gr fat-free cottage cheese(grainy)

- Optional for shaping:

- 2 tbsp cornstarch 40 gr (2 DOPs)

Directions:

1. Cut the onions into large pieces
2. Put the onion + egg into the blender bowl, chop until a homogeneous slurry
3. Grind cottage cheese until smooth.
4. If the volume of the blender bowl allows, put the cottage cheese immediately to the onion and egg and chop everything together. . If the bowl is small, leave a small part of the gruel in it, add cottage cheese, chop
5. Put minced meat, onion-egg gruel, cottage cheese in a bowl. Salt, add seasonings, herbs
6. Mix the minced meat well, at least 5 minutes.
7. Leave in the refrigerator to cool for 30 minutes
8. From the finished minced meat we form cutlets, roll in starch
9. If you want to save DOPs, just don't roll the cutlets, but fry them right away

10. 1 tsp oil for frying smear with a napkin on a frying pan, heat it up.
11. Fry cutlets until cooked on both sides

Cajun spice mix

Ingredients:

- 1 teaspoon ground black pepper
- 1 teaspoon onion powder
- 1 teaspoon cayenne pepper
- 1 ¼ teaspoons dried oregano
- 1 ¼ teaspoons dried thyme
- 2 teaspoons salt
- 2 teaspoons garlic powder
- 2 ½ teaspoons paprika
- ½ teaspoon red pepper flakes (optional)

Directions:

1. Stir together salt, garlic powder, paprika, black pepper, onion powder, cayenne pepper, oregano, thyme, and red pepper flakes until evenly blended. Store in an airtight container.

Grilled asparagus

Ingredients:

- 1 pound fresh asparagus spears, trimmed
- 1 tablespoon olive oil
- Salt and pepper to taste

Directions:

1. Preheat grill for high heat.
2. Lightly coat the asparagus spears with olive oil. Season with salt and pepper to taste.
3. Grill over high heat for 2 to 3 minutes, or to desired tenderness.

Dukan Bread

Ingredients:

- 1 Whole Egg

- 2 Egg whites

- 3 tablespoons of fat free Greek Yogurt

- 2 tablespoons of Oat bran

- 1 tablespoon of Wheat bran

- 1/2 pack of Yeast

Directions:

1. Beat the eggs in a microwavable bowl with the yogurt
2. Add the oat and wheat bran and yeast and mix well.

3. Allow the mixture to rise for around 30 minutes.
4. Microwave on full power for between 3 and 5 minutes depending on the thickness of mixture.
5. A mixture made in a shallower bowl will cook quicker than one made in a deeper bowl. You may need to experiment a little to get the timing right.
6. When cooked remove from bowl and allow to cool.
7. Slice in half and toast.

Fast And Easy Ginger Dukan Biscuits

Ingredients:

- 1 1/2 tablespoons of zero fat quark or fromage frais
- 1 1/2 teaspoons of dried ginger
- 4 beaten egg whites
- 3 tablespoons of oat bran
- Sweetener to taste

Directions:

1. Put the ginger, egg whites, bran, quark or fromage frais and sweetener in a bowl and mix together. The mixture needs to be thicker than the pancake.

2. Add a little of oil to your non stick frying pan and wipe the oil away using a piece of paper kitchen towel.
3. Instead of cooking as one pancake split make several smaller biscuit sized pancakes. Depending on how big your pan is and how big you like your biscuits you will probably have to cook 3 or 4 batches.
4. When browned turn your cookies and cook the other side.
5. Allow to cool before serving.

Shrimp And Grits With Tasso Ham

Ingredients:

- ½ diced Tasso ham

- 2 tablespoons diced onion

- 2 tablespoons diced green bell pepper

- 20 medium sized shrimps, peeled and deveined

- ¼ cup white wine

- Salt and ground pepper to taste

- 1 cup water

- 1 pinch salt

- 6 tablespoons grits

- 2 tablespoons olive oil

- 1 tablespoon chopped green onion, green parts only

Directions:

1. Prepare the grit mixture by allowing water and oil to boil. Once it has boiled, slowly add in the grits with constant stirring. Do this over low fire for about 20 minutes for thickened grits to be produced.
2. In a skillet, tossed up the tasso ham in preheated olive oil. Add onion and green pepper until onion is cooked. Add in the shrimp, and cook until pinkish. Set aside.
3. Using the skillet in which the ham was tossed, pour in the wine, and add salt and pepper.
4. Ladle the grits into separate bowls, and put at the center of a plate. Put the stir-fried shrimp on the edge of the plate. Top the grits with the wine mixture.

5. Serve, and enjoy!

Lemon Chicken Grilled

Ingredients:

- 2 tbsp finely chopped red bell pepper
- 2 large cloves garlic, finely chopped
- 1 tbsp Dijon mustard
- ¼ cup olive oil
- 4 skinless, boneless chicken breast halves
- ¼ tsp ground black pepper
- ½ tsp salt
- 1/3 cup lemon juice

Directions:

1. Combine pepper, salt, red bell pepper, garlic, dijon mustard, olive oil, and lemon juice in a bowl, and mix well.
2. To use as basting, keep in a separate bowl ¼ of the liquid mixture.
3. Add chicken into the mixture, and allow marinade to seep into the chicken for at least 20 minutes.
4. Oil the grate, and preheat grill to high fire.
5. Once grill is heated, add chicken, and cook for 6-8 minutes per side, or until juices run clear.
6. Every once in a while, baste chicken with reserve marinade.
7. Once chicken is cooked to desired completion, remove from grill, and serve.

Oat Bran Dukan Porridge

Ingredients:

- 4 tbsp. of milk powder, skim
- 2 egg whites from enormous eggs
- 2 tbsp. of sugar substitute
- 4 tbsp. of wheat, oat
- 10 1/2 liquid ounces of milk, skim

Directions:

1. Mix every one of your fixings aside from milk in breakfast measured bowl.
2. Add milk gradually and mix till there are no lumps.
3. Cook in microwave briefly and a half on 750 power level. Mix well.

4. Cook briefly more on 650 power level. Mix again.
5. Cook at one-minute spans on 650 till cooked completely. Serve.

Sausage Scramble With Jalapenos

Ingredients:

- 2 helpings of wiener, turkey

- 1/2 cut onion, small

- 2 eggs, large

- 3 huge egg whites

Directions:

1. Brown onion and hotdog in non-stick pan.
2. Add the eggs and join. Serve.

Candice's Modified Dukan Diet Chocolate Muffins

Ingredients:

- 2 tbsp oat bran
- 1/2 cup nonfat milk
- 1/2 cup xylitol (or any zero cal sweetener)
- 1 scoop chocolate whey protein powder (I like Amplify brand!)
- 1 tbsp baking powder
- 1/4 cup cocoa powder
- 1 egg

Directions:

1. Combine all the ingredients in a mixing bowl and blend until there are no lumps.
2. Pour batter into muffin tins.
3. Bake at 350 for 20-30 minutes. Check the middle with a toothpick or fork to ensure they are done!

Crispy Chicken

Ingredients:

- 250 grams of chicken breast (2 breasts)

- 1 egg white

- 2 tablespoons of oat bran breadcrumbs mixture (it should be 70% oat bran 30% breadcrumbs)

Directions:

1. Whisk the egg white well.
2. Put the oat bran and breadcrumbs mixture on a plate.
3. Cover the chicken first with the egg and then the breadcrumbs mixture and fry it in a pan without oil.

4. You can also add some skimmed milk to the liquid mixture if you want.

Meatballs in Tomato Sauce

Ingredients:

Meatballs

- 1 grated carrot

- 1 grated zucchini

- 1 tbsp Pesto

- 50g finely grated Parmesan

- 500g ground beef

- 2 cloves garlic, crushed

- 2 Eggs

- 4 tbsp oat bran

Tomato sauce

- 2 tins diced tomatoes
- 1 cup beef stock
- Freshly cracked black pepper
- 1 tsp olive oil
- 4 slices bacon (only the good round end part)
- 250g finely diced mushrooms
- Fresh basil (or dried)

Directions:

To make the meatballs:

1. Preheat oven to 180 degrees Celsius (360F).
2. Combine all Meatball Ingredients: in a large bowl and mix well with your hands to combine.
3. Roll tablespoon sized balls and place on a baking dish, evenly spread apart.

4. Bake for 40 minutes, turning half way.
5. Remove from the oven and place on some paper towel.

To make the tomato sauce:

6. Once the meatballs are in the oven. Heat the oil in a heavy bottomed pan. Add the onion and gently fry until translucent.
7. Add the Bacon and Mushrooms and fry until cooked.
8. When Onion, Bacon and Mushrooms are cooked, add the tins of Tomatoes, Beef Stock, Pepper and Basil. Bring to a simmer and slowly cook until meatballs are ready.
9. Add Meatballs to the Tomato Sauce and allow to cook over a low heat for a little while longer until sauce reduces. This is not an exact science, it just depends on how it looks in your kitchen.
10. Serve with some fresh basil.

Scallops In Ham Wrap

Ingredients:

- 3 tbsp. Wine, white

- ¼ Tsp. Pepper, black, ground

- 1 lb. scallops, large

- 4 oz. Prosciutto, sliced thinly

- 2 tbsp. Oil, olive

Directions:

1. Wrap the scallops in thin prosciutto slices. Secure them with toothpicks.
2. Heat oil in large sized skillet on med-high. Place scallops in pan. Then, cook for two or three minutes per side. Season both sides with the pepper while they cook.

3. Once both sides are fried, sprinkle wine over them. Cook for one or two additional minutes.
4. Remove scallops from pan. Then, allow to drain on plate lined with paper towels. When cooled a bit, transfer them to tray. Remove toothpicks and serve.

General Tso's Chicken

Ingredients:

- 1 minced garlic clove

- 2 stalks green onion, only the white part, cut small

- ½ Tbsp. Wine, shaoxing

- 1 pinch salt, kosher

- 1/3 c. Corn starch

- 10 oz. Bite-size cut chicken breast, skinless, boneless

- 5 de-seeded, rinsed, dried chilies, red

- Tso sauce, bottled

- 3 minced slices ginger, peeled

Directions:

1. Marinate chicken meat in kosher salt and Shaoxing wine for 12 to 15 minutes.
2. Generously coat chicken with corn starch. Heat non-stick pan. Fry chicken till it turns lighter brown. Remove chicken using strainer. Drain off excess fat onto paper towels.
3. Heat up skillet with 1 1/2 tbsp. of non-stick spray. Add chilies, ginger and garlic into skillet. Stir fry till you can easily smell the chilies' aroma.
4. Pour tso sauce into skillet. When it thickens and boils, add chicken. Combine by stirring with sauce. Add green onions. Stir several times. Serve hot in individual dishes.

Dukan Chili

Ingredients:

- 2 tbsp. Worcestershire sauce

- 1 ½ tsp. Cumin, ground

- 1 can undrained tomatoes, diced

- 1 tsp. Paprika, smoked

- 1 ½ lb. Chuck, ground

- 1 can undrained kidney beans

- 1 tsp. Salt, kosher

- ½ Tsp. Pepper, ground

- 1 c. Cheddar cheese shreds

- 1 can undrained pinto beans

- 1 c. Chopped bell pepper, green

- 7 oz. Broth, beef

- 1 chopped and de-seeded jalapeno

- 1 tbsp. Garlic, chopped

- 2 tbsp. Chili powder

- 6 oz. Tomato paste

- 1 ½ lb. onions, chopped

Directions:

1. Cook the ground chuck, onions, bell peppers, garlic and jalapeno in large sized pan on med-high heat for 8-10 minutes.
2. Crumble beef as you cook. It should not be pink at all when you're done. Stir the mixture occasionally and drain.

3. Add tomato paste, kosher salt, ground pepper, paprika, cumin and chili powder. Cook for a couple minutes until they are fragrant.
4. Add in and stir the Worcestershire sauce, undrained tomatoes and beans. Bring to boil and reduce heat.
5. Cover and simmer for 40-45 minutes, while you occasionally stir the mixture. Serve with the cheese.

www.ingramcontent.com/pod-product-compliance
Lightning Source LLC
LaVergne TN
LVHW010222070526
838199LV00062B/4694